Quote Octopus
Melbourne, Victoria, 3053
Australia
www.quoteoctopus.com

To the lover of wilderness, Alaska is one of the most wonderful countries in the world.

John Muir

The Bermuda Triangle got tired of warm weather. It moved to Alaska. Now Santa Claus is missing.

Steven Wright

It is easy to see what many people, women especially, admire about Sarah Palin. Here is a mother of five who can see the bright side of having a child with Down syndrome and still find the time and energy to govern the state of Alaska.

Sam Harris

For sheer majestic geography and sublime scale, nothing beats Alaska and the Yukon. For culture, Japan. And for all-around affection, Australia.

Sam Abell

Growing up in Alaska, they don't really teach you to swim there. I learned to swim just a few summers ago with Olympic gold medalist Amanda Beard. She did great, and right after that I went to get scuba certified. I had fun with it. I didn't really get scared, but some people thought that was a risk.

Holly Madison

Unless we make Christmas an occasion to share our blessings, all the snow in Alaska won't make it 'white'.

Bing Crosby

America is looking for answers. She's looking for a new direction; the world is looking for a light. That light can come from America's great North Star; it can come from Alaska.

Sarah Palin

It's not like Alaska isn't wilderness - it mostly is. But most Alaskans don't live in the wild. They live on the edge of the wild in towns with schools and cable TV and stores and dentists and roller rinks sometimes. It's just like anyplace else, only with mountains and moose.

Tom Bodett

In 1977, I climbed a fairly difficult mountain for the first time, which was Mount McKinley, in Alaska. I climbed the so-called 'American Direct Route,' which was a route straight up to the top. I really enjoyed it. Through such experiences, I learned that mountaineering wasn't just about height. I found that different routes have different charms.

Tamae Watanabe

Tom Kizzia hasn't just observed and written about Alaska for three-plus decades, he's lived it. 'Pilgrim's Wilderness' is a story that needed to be told by the only man who could tell it.

Tom Bodett

With the most powerful binoculars, I cannot see Alaska.

Mikheil Saakashvili

Historically, Alaska is a place that has attracted those fed up with conventionality.

Bill O'Reilly

A changing environment will affect Alaska more than any other state, because of our location. I'm not one though who would attribute it to being man-made.

Sarah Palin

The light in Alaska in particular is so beautiful. So beautiful! Such incredible light.

Sebastiao Salgado

Alaska is what happens when Willy Wonka and the witch from Hansel and Gretel elope, buy a place together upstate, renounce their sweet teeth, and turn into health fanatics.

Sloane Crosley

Alaska itself is an unusual state.

Fareed Zakaria

Sarah Palin, who with 17 months remaining in her single term as Alaska's governor quit the only serious office she has ever held, is obsessively discussed as a possible candidate in 2012. Why? She is not going to be president and will not be the Republican nominee unless the party wants to lose at least 44 states.

George Will

Kids in Alaska don't know they're growing up on the Last Frontier. It's just what they see on the license plates, and it's something tourists like to say a lot because they've never been around so many mountains and moose before.

Tom Bodett

There was really no friendship in modeling, though a certain amount of warmth comes from running into models you know on shoots, because you end up in so many unfamiliar places, from Alaska to Africa.

Carol Alt

I've always been fascinated and stared at maps for hours as a kid. I've especially been most intrigued by the uninhabited or lonelier places on the planet. Like Greenland, for instance, or just recently flying over Alaska and a chain of icy, mountainous islands, uninhabited.

Andrew Bird

I'm not someone who can lie on a beach and do nothing. I am not sure what you are supposed to do, so I get bored. I prefer to have a purpose, such as going to Alaska to see orca whales.

Miranda Richardson

There's a lot of people around Alaska now who are actually running the place who claim to just have gone there for the summer once 30 years ago. And that seems to be what happens.

Tom Bodett

Many climate scientists say their biggest fear is that warming could melt the Arctic permafrost - which stretches for thousands of miles across Alaska, Canada, and Siberia.

Michael Specter

Since 2006, we have surpassed Alaska, Oklahoma, Louisiana, and California in oil production to become the second largest oil-producing state in the nation, trailing only Texas. In 2012,

North Dakota produced more than 245 million barrels of oil and provided nearly 11 percent of all U.S. output.

John Hoeven

I like Alaska for the salmon fishing - it's fantastic there. I usually stay in a log cabin with no one around for miles. I like to go with friends, but I'm also happy to be on my own with nature.

Vinnie Jones

I served at the Pentagon and at Fort Leavenworth - my job was video cameraman, and that allowed me to travel to places like Korea, Japan, Alaska, Germany and the Netherlands.

Chad Coleman

Alaska and Montana are not in the south but they definitely form part of the crimson tide of red states where Republicans are dominant.

Juan Williams

This was one of the places people told me to go, it was one the big trips that you should see: Alaska.

Jeff Goldblum

When oil and gas prices went up dramatically and filled up the state treasury, I sent a large share of that revenue back where it belonged - directly to the people of Alaska.

Sarah Palin

I've always heard that heli-skiing in Alaska is amazing. I would love to be able to do that at some point in my life.

Lindsey Vonn

Once a popular Alaska governor with a modest record of accomplishment, Palin could conceivably revive her reputation in this era of short memories. But it's hard to imagine her name atop the GOP ballot in 2016, when a cast of heavyweights who sat out 2012 will be vying for the nomination.

Ron Fournier

I went to Alaska as a young man just looking for adventure. And like so many of us in the '70s, we found it.

Tom Bodett

I think we should drill up in Alaska.

Joe Barton

John Muir, the famous naturalist, wrote in his journal that you should never go to Alaska as a young man because you'll never be satisfied with any other place as long as you live. And there's a lot of truth to that.

Tom Bodett

I was so grateful to have made 'Into the Wild' before I made 'Speed Racer' because on 'Speed Racer' I was indoors every single day, every single scene, on a green screen. Some of the time, just to pass the time, I would think back to climbing mountains in Alaska. That really helped me.

Emile Hirsch

We should start by allowing drilling in Alaska's National Wildlife Refuge. It can provide billions of barrels of recoverable oil and trillions of cubic feet of recoverable natural gas.

Mac Thornberry

The state of Alaska has a minimum wage which is higher than the federal level because our state leaders have made that determination.

Joe Miller

Since my parents both worked, they hired me when I was 11 to make dinner every night. I got a quarter a day. But I was always making things like duck a l'orange and baked Alaska. I was a little bit nutty.

Teri Hatcher

Mitt Romney understands the importance of Alaska as a leader in our country's energy production and I look forward to working with him on such an important economic and national security matter.

Lisa Murkowski

Walter, who had been in the lead all day, was the first to scramble up; a native Alaskan, he is the first human being to set foot upon the top of Alaska's great mountain, and he had well earned the lifelong distinction.

Hudson Stuck

We've been helping you out in Alaska in considerable ways, and you're walking away from the responsibility, and we're not going to allow that.

Lisa Murkowski

What I miss most about living in Alaska is the fishing.

Darby Stanchfield

Laws made in Alaska, which is known for its lawlessness, are as valid as laws made in Pennsylvania, which invented laws.

Kevin Bleyer

But again, you know, the views that we've expressed are transferring power back from the federal government to the states, giving Alaska an incredible opportunity to expand its economy, especially at a time when our federal government is coming close to bankruptcy.So that is a broad-based appeal. It's not an extreme view.

Joe Miller

I never watch MTV. I don't have time to watch TV. And when I do, I'm watching the Discovery Channel. 'Deadliest Catch: Crab Fishing in Alaska,' that's my show.

Carly Schroeder

There are many outsiders that actively try to halt every natural resource development project in Alaska. Many of these same people have never even been to Alaska, yet they claim to know what's best for us.

Lisa Murkowski

I missed that question on Alaska. I hear they want to make it a state now.

Anson Williams

In one line of his poem he said good fences make good neighbors. I'd like to think that Alaska and British Columbia working together can prove that we can be pretty darned good neighbors without fences.

Dan Miller

I'm thankful for Sarah Palin's vice presidential bid, which taught us that Alaska is not in a box off the coast of California.

Paula Poundstone

The original settlers of Alaska apparently were Russian.

Jeff Goldblum

In more than 500 instances, from the Gulf of Alaska to Bar Harbor, Maine, FEMA has remapped waterfront properties from the highest-risk flood zone, saving the owners as much as 97 percent on the premiums they pay into the financially strained National Flood Insurance Program.

Bill Dedman

'Not again!' I thought to myself this morning, as news trickled out that John McCain was set to pick Alaska governor Sarah

Palin as his running mate. Not again, because too often women are promoted for the wrong reasons, and then blamed when things don't go right.

Dee Dee Myers

Alaska Airlines and I have a lot in common, so coming together to delight travelers with savory, high quality food from the Pacific Northwest made sense.

Tom Douglas

In the 1970s, 'The Boys on the Bus' exposed how a clubby pack of male political reporters ruled the road to the White House and shaped the news. Four decades later, an outsider gal from Alaska has commandeered the 2012 media bus - and left Beltway journalism insiders eating her dust.

Michelle Malkin

The Maldives, a string of islands off the coast of India whose highest point above sea level is eight feet, may be the first nation to drown. In Alaska, entire towns have begun to shift in the loosening permafrost.

Michael Specter

I'm about to do my second Bikram yoga class in Anchorage, Alaska. It's the only way to stay warm. I've got to get into shape. I've been eating nothing but fish and chips.

Emily Blunt

I don't think I can tell any stories about how I lived in a van in Alaska. I grew up in the suburbs, I even had my own room. We weren't poor. Everything was very normal.

Lisa Loeb

We can get more energy out of the north slope of Alaska; we have available the ability to make ourselves less dependent on those uncertain sources of supply from the Middle East. And it's important we do that.

John W. Snow

Really, I didn't like Alaska. It rained, almost every day, at least 300 days out of the year.

John C. Hawkes

When we lived in Juneau, Alaska, it was a town of about 7,000 people, and totally isolated; the only way to get to it was by ship.

John C. Hawkes

Why would even I say we can't stop drilling in the Gulf? Because we have no alternatives. Whether or not we drill in the Gulf, or in Alaska, we will continue to wring the last out of anyplace else.

Carl Safina

I've had a lot of crappy jobs, but one of my favorites was working as a commercial fisherman in Alaska. What I loved about it was, you got paid for what you caught.

Jon Krakauer

When I was 23, I went to Alaska by myself into the glaciers of the coast range and climbed a mountain by myself. It was incredibly reckless, incredibly stupid. But I was lucky. And I survived, and I came back to tell my story.

Jon Krakauer

We host some trips all over the world. We go to Alaska. We go to Mexico. We're going to Venezuela in December. We've been to Russia, all in conjunction with the radio show.

Martin Milner

What is good for Alaska is good for the country. Transferring power from the federal government to the states provides opportunity to all states, not just Alaska.

Joe Miller

If the world were an orange with 18 segments meeting at the top (the North Pole), roughly 8 of them would be in Russia, Canada would have 4, Denmark 2, and Norway, Sweden, and the U.S. just one apiece. Only a sliver of Alaska, on the Beaufort Sea, lies above the Arctic Circle.

Alex Shoumatoff

I'm for catching every Japanese in America, Alaska, and Hawai'i now and putting them in concentration camps.

Francis Biddle

I'm born in Alaska, grew up in Colorado, went to college in Colorado, went to Colorado State, and I actually finished my degree.

Derek Theler

I chose to document the lives of people living in a remote village in Alaska called Shishmaref because there we can literally see how climate change is affecting their homes, livelihoods and ultimately their lives.

Amy J. Berg

Bears are extremely human, even down to their footprints. But I am also a fly fisherman, so I have fished beside brown bears in Alaska and was once charged by a black bear. I love bears.

Joseph Monninger

Let's not get caught up in the D.C. trap of Democrats versus Republicans. When you're in Alaska it's about what's important for Alaska.

Mark Begich

Alaska has great potential for new oil and gas development.

Frank Murkowski

One of Alaska's strengths is our pioneer role in environmentally sensitive development.

Frank Murkowski